Robert Bennet Forbes

An Interesting Memoir of the Jamestown Voyage to Ireland

Robert Bennet Forbes

An Interesting Memoir of the Jamestown Voyage to Ireland

ISBN/EAN: 9783742809643

Manufactured in Europe, USA, Canada, Australia, Japa

Cover: Foto ©ninafisch / pixelio.de

Manufactured and distributed by brebook publishing software
(www.brebook.com)

Robert Bennet Forbes

An Interesting Memoir of the Jamestown Voyage to Ireland

AN INTERESTING MEMOIR

OF THE

JAMESTOWN VOYAGE TO IRELAND.

BY THE LATE

R. B. FORBES.

ILLUSTRATED.

PUBLISHERS' ANNOUNCEMENT.

THE publishers present herewith a unique bit of literature to the public, and add it to the historical collections already in the archives of Massachusetts.

This authentic memoir is from the pen of the late Capt. Forbes, in his day one of the worthiest and best respected citizens of Boston.

The contents of the book are of solid value, and of interest to everybody.

America and Ireland are old, tried, true, and loyal friends; these two nations are united in bonds of love and sympathy which have been strengthened by all the terrors of adversity and the dreadful sacrifice of human life for a common cause. To-day, the international influences wielded by the Irish people have become potent factors in shaping foreign affairs, and the sustaining power of the Irish people in this country is the life of the Republic.

Any event which has alternately made a beneficiary of either the American or the Irish nation is of world-wide interest.

* In 1676, Ireland sent supplies to the starving colonists of Massachusetts, and the voyage of the "Jamestown," one hundred and seventy years later, was a practical demonstration of the gratitude of the American people. The story is well told in the following pages by the noble American commander who guided the vessel on her errand of mercy into the Irish port, during that eventful famine-stricken period.

By a special request of the publishers, Capt. Forbes wrote this succinct story. No more fitting time to pay a just tribute to his memory has come than the present, since his demise is of recent occurrence.

We are convinced that the professional man, the merchant, the mechanic, and a large class of people who will not purchase exhaustive and costly works will bid this piece of condensed historical information a hearty welcome.

THE PUBLISHERS.

* See "The Story of the Irish in Boston," Cullen, pages 79, 80, and 81.

SYNOPSIS OF CONTENTS.

Washington's birthday, 1847. — Congress petitioned on behalf of Ireland. — A joint resolution passed. — The frigate "Macedonian" loaned. — The sloop-of-war "Jamestown." — On St. Patrick's Day the Laborers' Aid Society stores about one thousand tons of supplies on board. — Sunday, March 28. — The start for sea. — The Boston Relief Committee. — The tug "R. B. Forbes." — Capt. F. W. Macondray. — Capt. James Dumaresq Farwell. — Dr. Luther Parks. — The crew of the "Jamestown." — A sketch of the ship. — The Rev. R. C. Waterston calls attention to Ireland's aid to America in 1676. — An account of the "Irish donation." — Mr. Waterston's grateful tribute to Ireland's charity. — "Cast thy bread upon the waters, for thou shall find it after many days." — "A ship-of-war changed into an angel of mercy." — "She carries with her the best wishes of millions." — The blessing. — The amount of the contributions of Irishmen to America in 1676. — "We have planted in the Irish heart a debt which will come back to us in the future, bearing fruit crowned with peace and good-will." — Capt. Forbes relates the particulars of the voyage. — Good by, Boston Light. — Queenstown, ho! — A visit from Lieut.-Commander Trotheral, of Her Majesty's ship "Crocodile." — A message from Rear Admiral Sir Hugh Pigot. — A deputation from the citizens of Cove of Cork. — The band begins to play. — Cork illuminated. — The meeting of Capt. Forbes and Father Mathew. — They proceed to Cork together. — A banquet at the Cove. — A dinner on the "Crocodile." — Capt. Forbes meets the Temperance Institute at Cork. — Father Mathew presides. — Irish ladies. — Nine days at Cork. — Capt. Forbes "at home," from twelve to three, to the residents of Cork and Cove. — He entertains several hundred by music from Father Mathew's Temperance Band, a barrel of Welsh best ship-bread, flanked by ice from Fresh Pond, lemonade, and a sample of Mrs. Mayer's hard gingerbread. — Irish ladies dance with the red-coats and blue-coats on the deck of the ship. — Presented with a portrait of Father Mathew. — Capt. Forbes invites him to Boston. — Obliged to stay with his famine-stricken countrymen. — An incident. — An English lord applies to Capt. Forbes for relief. — The Captain's reply. — Good by to old Ireland. — Passing Spike Island. — The Royal Marines give three cheers. — The American flag makes response. — Admiral Pigot and the "Zephyr." — "Keep her as long as her coal lasts." — Man overboard. Lost! — The "Macedonian." — The cost of the voyage. — Report of the Relief Committee. — Receipts and expenses of the voyage.

A SKETCH

OF THE

HISTORY OF THE JAMESTOWN VOYAGE.

ON the twenty-second day of February, 1847, certain merchants of Boston forwarded to the Hon. R. C. Winthrop a petition asking Congress to loan a United States ship to carry to Ireland a cargo of supplies for the famine-stricken people of Ireland. On the third of March, the last stormy day of the session, Congress passed a joint resolution granting the loan of the frigate "Macedonian" to Capt. Geo. C. DeKay, of New York, and the sloop-of-war "Jamestown" to myself, as I happened to have headed the said petition, and the Hon. J. T. Mason, Secretary of the Navy, at once sent an order to Com. F. A. Parker, commandant of the Navy Yard at Charlestown, to prepare the "Jamestown" by the removal of her armament.

The order came on the eleventh of March, and on St. Patrick's Day, the seventeenth, the Laborers' Aid Society stowed on board about one thousand tons of stores; by the twenty-seventh she was full, say about eight thousand barrels in bulk, consisting of provisions, grain, meal, clothing, etc.

On Sunday, the twenty-eighth, at 8.30 A. M., the fasts were cast off, and with a fine breeze at northwest, we started for sea, accompanied by the tow-boat "R. B. Forbes," on board of which were the Boston Relief Committee, consisting of Hon. Josiah Quincy, Jr., chairman, Thomas Lee, J. Ingersoll

Bowditch, James K. Mills, Geo. W. Crockett, and Hon. David Henshaw.

In about an hour the committee came near and requested me to heave to and put out the pilot, Mr. Phillips, but I returned for answer that the tug must come close to the quarter and he would be swung on board with the aid of the vang of the spanker gaff. This was done successfully, and with hearty cheers from the committee we proceeded on our way.

It may be well here to state that my chief officer was Capt. F. W. Macondray, who had been several years in my employ; my second officer was Capt. James Dumaresq Farwell, who had also been in my employ, volunteers without pay; and two experienced seamen, Messrs. White and ——, who were under pay. Dr. Luther Parks went as surgeon, and a young man by the name of Sullivan went as passenger, as an acknowledgment of his father's free services, as broker, in gathering together the cargo. Of active men fit to go aloft there were thirty-one, there were two stewards, a cook and his aid, and the balance, to make up the whole company to forty-nine all told, consisted of several green hands and several men who had become cripples from frosted feet.

The ship drew about twenty feet of water; the lower hold was full of cargo; the between decks, or what is called the "berth deck," where the crew and officers lived when she was a vessel-of-war, was also full of cargo, and the gun deck, covered in by a light "spar deck," was occupied by the crew and stores, by the launch and cutter, and by the pumps; my cabin and dining-room, with the quarters for the officers, occupied the after end of this deck; all the ports were planked up and made tight, but as the pumps still delivered their water on this deck and much came in through the rudder casing or port, this gun deck was constantly wet and uncomfortable. While fit-

ting out the ship, the Rev. R. C. Waterston wrote to me, stating that the records of Plymouth County showed that we received aid from Ireland in our infancy as a nation. I quote the following from the records of 1676 : —

" The order and distribution of this Colony's contributions made by divers Christians in Ireland, for the relief of such as are impoverished and distressed by the Indian wars, was, as respects this Colony, apportioned as followeth : — *

Appointed to distribute It.

PLYMOUTH	08	00	00	Leift. Morton. Joseph Warren. William Crow.
DUXBURROW	02	00	00	Mr. Josiah Standish. William Paybody.
SCITTUATE	12	00	00	Major Cudworth. Cornette Studson. Edward Jenkins.
TAUNTON	10	00	00	William Harvey. James Walker. John Richmond.
SWANSEY	21	00	00	Mr. Brown. John Butterworth.
MIDDLE BERRY	01	10	00	Francis Combe. Isacke Howard.
EASTHAM	00	10	00	Capt. Freeman.
YARMOUTH	00	10	00	Mr. John Thacher.
BARNSTABLE	03	00	00	Mr. Huckens. Barnabas Laythrop.
DARTMOUTH	22	00	00	John Cooke. John Smith. John Russell.
REHOBOTH	32	00	00	Mr. Nathaniel Paine. Lieft. Hunt. Mr. Daniell Smith.
MARSHFEILD	02	00	00	Ensigne Eames. Anthony Snow.
BRIDGWATER	07	00	00	Elder Brett. Deacon Willis. Mr. Samuel Edson."

* The amount, according to Morton's " New England Memorial," edited by Judge Davis, pages 459–61, was £124 10s., made to fourteen towns on the Cape.

To borrow the words of Mr. Waterston, I quote : " It is an interesting fact that the people of Ireland, nearly two hundred years ago, thus sent relief to our Pilgrim Fathers in the time of their need, and what we have been doing for that famishing country is but a return for what their fathers did for our fathers ; and the whole circumstances prove a verification of the Scripture, ' Cast thy bread upon the waters, for thou shalt find it after many days.'" In making this Scriptural quotation, Mr. Waterston goes on to say : " I consider the mission of the ' Jamestown' as one of the grandest events in the history of our country. A ship-of-war changed into an angel of mercy, departing on no errand of death, but with the bread of life to an unfortunate and perishing people. She carries with her the best wishes of millions, and it seemed as if Heaven smiled upon you in your speedy passage out and your safe return." It will readily be seen that these good and grateful words were not uttered until the voyage was ended.

In allusion to what the reverend friend had said, I remark, in the introduction to the history of the voyage of the " Jamestown," that I was very grateful to him for so successfully enabling me to weigh anchor, and complete the report to the Relief Committee.

The amount of the contributions of Irishmen in 1676, at compound interest, would be so large that I dare not say how much we should still be indebted after all New England has done and is doing.

The amount would be over $200,000. Let us hope to pay it off, still leaving us much in debt to Ireland ; we have planted in the Irish heart a debt which will come back to us in the future, bearing fruit crowned with peace and good-will.

After this preface, I will go on and give such particulars of the voyage as may be of interest to the present generation.

After taking leave of the Relief Committee off Boston Light, we were favored by a good run clear of George's Shoals and clear of the Banks, until, on the twelfth of April, fifteen days and three hours from home, we cast anchor in the outer harbor of what has since been known as Queenstown. We soon received a visit from Lieut.-Commander Trotheral, of Her Majesty's ship "Crocodile," conveying a message of welcome from Rear Admiral Sir Hugh Pigot, and an assurance that everything would be done to expedite the delivery of our cargo and to prepare the ship for her return to the United States. Early the following day the "Sabrina," Capt. Parker, a passenger steamer, came along, took us in tow, and carried us to the government store-houses at Haulbowline; before the ship was fairly moored, there came a deputation from the citizens of Cove of Cork, who had previously sent on board a band of music. On the thirteenth the town was illuminated; on the fourteenth the cargo was being discharged, and I proceeded to Cork, in company with Father Mathew, and was introduced to the collector and other officials on the fifteenth; a banquet was given by the citizens of Cove in honor of myself and my officers, and on the sixteenth I was entertained by a dinner on board of the "Crocodile." On the nineteenth I met the Temperance Institute at Cork, at the head of which Father Mathew presided: many were the kind words spoken on this occasion, and a number of short poems were presented by the ladies present; among others one came from Joseph Hamilton, Esq., of Dublin.

Considering that we were at Cork only nine days, it is a wonder that the spirit of song and poetry should have been awakened at all.

On the twenty-first of April, *twenty-four days only from leaving Boston,* I was "at home" from twelve to three to the residents of Cork and Cove, and I entertained several hundred

THE JAMESTOWN.

by music from Father Mathew's Temperance Band, and by a barrel of Welsh best ship-bread, flanked by a large piece of ice from Fresh Pond, which I declared was manufactured *expressly for the purpose* on the twenty-fifth of March. I gave also good lemonade, and a very small sample of Mrs. Mayer's hard gingerbread ; but it must be owned that the best part of the picnic was furnished by the ladies, who danced with the red-coats and the blue-coats on the deck of the ship.

On the twentieth of April I visited various officials, to take leave. On the twenty-second I went to Cork and made final arrangements with my kind friend and agent, Mr. William Rathbone, of Liverpool, for the distribution of my cargo and other cargoes coming to my consignment.

While at Cork, Mr. John O'Connor presented to me a portrait of Father Mathew, and an engraving of a tower erected to the memory of that good man, whom I invited to come with me to Boston, but he was obliged to decline, not wishing to leave his famine-stricken countrymen.

My agents at Cork were Messrs. N. & I. Cummins, and at Cove, Messrs. James Scott & Co., to whom I was much indebted for many acts of kindness and for free work in aid of my mission. Among the incidents of my stay at Cork, I might mention the application of Lord —— for relief; but on being asked to visit a fine yacht that he was building, I concluded that I might find better objects on whom to lodge any part of my cargo.

Finally, on the twenty-second of April, at 3.30 P. M., we left Cove in tow of Her Majesty's steamship "Zephyr." On passing Spike Island, where the Royal Marines, under Lieut.-Col. Coryton, were stationed, we were much gratified by seeing the whole corps drawn up under arms, and as we passed, they gave three cheers in a style never before experienced by me.

York to see how this could be done. It was determined to put
into her about five thousand barrels, and the Rev. Father
Taylor to go out in her in charge of the bill of lading. This
was done, and some time in June this cargo was landed at
the Cove of Cork, and Capt. DeKay went to Scotland and
landed his original two thousand five hundred barrels, returning
to New York in October.

The cost of the "Macedonian's" voyage was such that Capt.
DeKay went to Congress for relief, and procured a grant of
money to help out his expenses ; but he sacrificed much in the
good cause, and died not long after his return.

The report of the Relief Committee gives the following fig-
ures, receipts being, —

From Massachusetts .	. $115,041 96
Maine .	9,881 03
New Hampshire	18,401 38
Vermont .	4,371 02
Rhode Island .	1,030 50
Connecticut	1,068 00
Indiana .	223 16
Wisconsin	216 25
Illinois	20 00
Arkansas	153 75
	$150,407 05

Nearly $122,000 of this sum was received in cash. The city
of Boston gave $51,641.19 in cash and $521.75 in provisions ;
total, $52,162.94. Other Massachusetts towns gave $63,479.02.
The committee forwarded the contributions by the following
vessels : —

Steamer "Cambria" to Liverpool .	$1,085	00
United States ship "Jamestown" to Cork .	40,018	80
Bark "Tartar" for Cork .	29,752	23
Ship "Morea" for Glasgow	23,609	95
Ship "Reliance" for Cork . . .	27,946	37
United States ship "Macedonian" for Cork	23,840	94
Ship "Mary Ann" for Liverpool	181	13
Balance remitted by steamer	4,872	63
	$151,307	05

Railroads brought freight free, Bancroft trucked goods free, wharfage free, and the principal papers advertised free ; market men gave tons of food ; Hittinger gave ice.

The account of the voyage was as here stated : —

J. I. Bowditch, *Treasurer, in account with* R. B. Forbes.

1847.

June 12. To cash paid for

Provisions	$703	35
Wages of crew .	1,675	00
Lining water-tanks	60	31
Coopering cargo	14	78
Ship-chandlery .	44	73
Sundry expenses . .	34	25
Paid female employment, etc., at Cork, £40, and handed to J. Scott, at Cork, £60,	457	64
	$2,990	06

1847.

March 23.	Received of Treasurer	$800	00
26.	Received of Treasurer	664	90
April 5.	Received of Treasurer	1,180	19
June 14.	Received of Treasurer	20	16
	Passengers from Cork	107	61
	Ballast sold . . .	150	00
	Donation from S. C. Phillips .	33	60
	Donation from O. Goodwin	33	60
		$2,990	06

Errors excepted.

R. B. FORBES.

Boston, June 14, 1847.

Memorandum of the expenses of the voyage.

Provisions		$703 35
Wages .		1,675 00
Chandlery		44 73
Disbursements .		34 25
		$2,457 33

CR.

2 passengers	$107 61	
Ballast sold . . .	150 00	
2 men's wages found . . .	67 20	
Bill of provisions returned Winchester .	421 00	
		745 81
		$1,711 52

And contributed by the Boston churches on the day of sailing .	$3,076 64
Charges .	1,711 52
Balance	$1,365 12

This represents the amount of credit to committee, showing that *nothing was paid out*, and this amount was procured, over expenses.

R. B. FORBES.